CELEBRATING HANUKKAH

CELEBRATING

HANUKKAH

History, Traditions, and Activities
A HOLIDAY BOOK FOR KIDS

By Stacia Deutsch

Illustrations by Annita Soble

ROCKRIDGE
PRESS

First Rockridge Press trade paperback edition 2022

Rockridge Press and the Rockridge Press logo are trademarks or registered trademarks of Callisto Media Inc. and/or its affiliates in the United States and other countries and may not be used without written permission.

For general information on our other products and services, please contact our Customer Care Department within the United States at (866) 744-2665, or outside the United States at (510) 253-0500.

Hardcover ISBN: 979-8-88650-431-6 | Paperback ISBN: 978-1-68539-870-5
eBook ISBN: 979-8-88608-000-1

Manufactured in the United States of America

Series Designer: Elizabeth Zuhl
Interior and Cover Designer: Carlos Esparza
Art Producer: Janice Ackerman
Editor: Laura Apperson
Production Editor: Nora Milman
Production Manager: Lanore Coloprisco

Illustrations © 2022 Annita Soble
Pattern used under license from Shutterstock.com
Author photo courtesy of Val Westover

10 9 8 7 6 5 4 3 2 1 0

To my ancestors.

CONTENTS

WHAT IS HANUKKAH?

anukkah is a **Jewish** holiday that is also called the Festival of Lights. It lasts for eight nights during November or December. The holiday celebrates the victory of the Jewish people over the Greeks more than two thousand years ago. The Jewish people weren't allowed into their Holy Temple in Jerusalem, but after a mighty battle, a small group of Jewish fighters won the Temple back. They made the Temple holy again with a service called "re-dedication," where they re-lit the golden **menorah**. The word *Hanukkah* means "dedication" in **Hebrew**.

For thousands of years, Jewish people have celebrated Hanukkah by lighting candles and chanting prayers. Hanukkah can be celebrated alone or with family and friends. Before the candles are lit, people say blessings. After, they sing holiday songs. It's common to give presents to each other and donations to charity. Special foods and games add to the fun.

There can be differences in how Jewish people celebrate based on where their families come from. But for Jews everywhere, Hanukkah celebrates freedom, strength, and survival against the odds.

HISTORY AND FOLKLORE

Jewish people have celebrated Hanukkah for generations, and yet, there are many traditions still open for discussion. First is the name of the holiday. There are more than twenty ways to spell Hanukkah in English, including Chanukah, Hanukka, or Chanukkah. The spellings all come from the Hebrew word *Hanukkah* (חנוכה). There are many ways to pronounce it, too. In English, the holiday has an H sound at the beginning. But in Hebrew it is pronounced with a throaty KH sound, like a snore that goes out instead of in: "kha-nu-kah." There are different opinions about where the holiday came from, as well.

RULED BY OTHERS

Our current calendar starts with the year zero. Anything before that is considered BCE, or Before the Common Era. After zero is CE, or the Common Era. Around 200 BCE, the land of Judaea was ruled by a

Seleucid king named Antiochus III (an-TAI-uh-kuhs). Antiochus III allowed Jewish people who lived in his kingdom to practice their own religion, **Judaism**. When Antiochus's son, Antiochus IV, became king, it was clear that he was different from his father. Antiochus IV made Judaism **illegal**. He wanted Jewish people to worship Greek gods. (The Greek people worshipped many gods, whereas the Jewish people worshipped only one God.) In 168 BCE, Antiochus's soldiers went to Jerusalem to change the Jews' Holy Temple into a place to worship Zeus, a Greek god. The Jewish people were afraid. Many followed the king's orders and gave up their faith. But one family said no. They decided to fight against King Antiochus and his mighty army.

THE HAMMER

Mattathias the Hasmonean (mat-uh-TAI-uhs the haz-muh-NEE-uhn) was a Jewish religious leader who lived near the city of Jerusalem. In 167 BCE, Mattathias and his five sons declared that they were going to take back the Temple.

Mattathias, his family, and other **rebels** hid in the hills. They battled the king's soldiers. They also fought against other Jewish people who were following the king's rules.

When Mattathias died, his middle son became the group's leader. He was known as Judah Maccabee. The word *maccabee* means "hammer" in Hebrew. Judah was known to strike the king's soldiers in short, quick blows, just like a hammer. Soon, all the rebels were called Maccabees.

The Maccabees fought hard. It took three years, but in 164 BCE they finally reclaimed the Temple in Jerusalem.

THE SECOND TEMPLE OF JERUSALEM

King David was a ruler of ancient Israel. According to the **Bible**, he planned to build a temple in Jerusalem. He didn't live long enough to do it. Instead, in 957 BCE, his son Solomon built the Holy Temple. Jewish people worshipped there for a long time. Then, in 586 BCE, Nebuchadnezzar II (neh·buh·kuhd·neh·zr) of Babylonia conquered the area and destroyed it. The Jewish people were forced to leave.

In 583 BCE, a new ruler, Cyrus II of Persia, let the people rebuild. This Second Temple was once again the center of Jewish life, until King Antiochus took it over in 168 BCE. The Maccabees eventually defeated Antiochus's soldiers and reclaimed the Temple. Later, in 20 BCE, King Herod expanded the Holy Temple, but the Romans destroyed it in 70 CE.

Today, Jewish people still pray at the one remaining wall of Jerusalem's ancient Holy Temple.

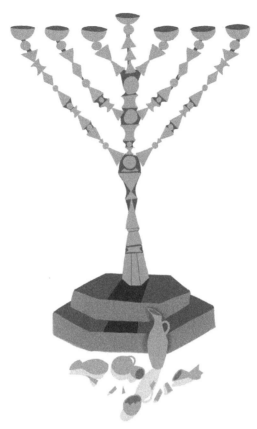

THE HANUKKAH MIRACLE

Inside the Holy Temple, there was a golden menorah, a seven-branched **candelabra**. In Jewish belief, it was important that the flames of this menorah burn all the time because the light represented God's presence.

The **Talmud** is one of Judaism's most important texts. It says that when the Maccabees entered the Temple, they discovered that Antiochus's soldiers had let the flames of the sacred menorah go out.

The Maccabees needed to rekindle the flames with oil. But there was only enough oil for one day. It would take eight days to get more.

That's when a great miracle happened. That little bit of oil burned continuously for eight days, until more oil arrived. The light of God's presence once again filled the Temple. It was time to celebrate!

OTHER ORIGINS OF HANUKKAH

Why do Jewish people celebrate Hanukkah? Most people say it's because of the miracle that the oil lasted eight days. There are others, however, who say the miracle isn't real.

The history of the Maccabees' rebellion was written in texts called the Books of the Maccabees. These four books were written closest to the time the war happened. There's no miracle mentioned in the Books of the Maccabees, but it does say there was a celebration for eight days and nights after the Maccabees' victory. It's possible that Hanukkah is not celebrated because of a miracle, but instead because the Maccabees won the fight for the Temple.

Historically, it's true that the story about the amazing oil was first written down nearly 700 years after the Maccabees' battle.

There's another theory. Some historians think that the story of the Maccabees was not really about the Jewish people fighting King Antiochus at all. Instead, they believe there was a civil war between different **sects** of Jewish people. It was a battle to decide which sect got to choose the **high priest** of the Jewish people. The Maccabees won, and perhaps they created Hanukkah to celebrate their own personal victory.

CELEBRATING SUKKOT

There is one other explanation about the origins of Hanukkah. This one is different from all the others.

In the autumn season, there is a Jewish celebration called **Sukkot**, which, along with an added holiday, is celebrated for eight days. Some people believe that King Antiochus took over the Temple during this holiday. When the Jewish people got the Temple back, they celebrated Sukkot. They had missed it during Antiochus's invasion. The Second Book of Maccabees describes the rededication ceremony at the Temple. The description includes a lot of Sukkot's rituals, like carrying palm fronds and offering hymns of thanks to God.

Today's Hanukkah celebration takes bits from each of the origin stories: a lot of oil, a gathering for eight nights, a victory in battle, and a party to celebrate the survival of the Jewish people.

Pure olive oil was used in the Temple menorah. The olives were picked, washed, pitted, and crushed. Oil was then carefully separated from the fruit pulp. This was all done by hand.

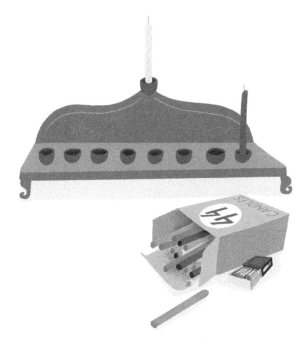

PREPARING FOR HANUKKAH

Just like there isn't only one story for the origin of Hanukkah, there isn't only one way to celebrate, either! There are a lot of different Hanukkah customs and ways to participate in the holiday.

WHAT IS A MENORAH?

Officially, a menorah has seven branches. The one used for Hanukkah has nine. It is also known as a

hanukkiah, but the word *menorah* is commonly used for both. For Hanukkah, the ninth candle, called a **shamash**, is lit first. The shamash is then used to kindle each of the other eight lights. *Shamash* means "helper" in Hebrew.

According to tradition, the candles all need to be in a row except for the shamash. It can be in front, behind, above, or below the other candles. Some Hanukkah menorahs look like small versions of the menorah in the Holy Temple. Some are fancy works of art, look like animals, or have sports themes. Some menorahs use oil and **wicks** instead of candles. Others use light bulbs.

No matter what the menorah looks like, it's fun to light the candles and celebrate Hanukkah!

THE CANDLES OF HANUKKAH

Can you figure out how many candles are needed for all of Hanukkah? To find the answer, there are a few important things you need to know.

1. The shamash, or the helper candle, should always be lit first. Then it is used to light the other candles in the menorah.
2. It is tradition to let the candles burn all night during Hanukkah. This means the menorah is set up with new candles every night.
3. Here's the math: On the first night, you light the shamash and the first candle. That makes two. On the second night, you light the shamash and two candles. That makes three. This continues for eight nights. Now add it all up.

You can find the world's tallest Hanukkah menorah in New York City's Grand Army Plaza in Manhattan. It's 32 feet high and weighs nearly 4,000 pounds.

So, how many candles will you need to celebrate eight nights of Hanukkah? Turn to page 19 to find out!

MAKING DINNER

A lot of popular Hanukkah foods are fried in oil. This honors the miracle of the oil in the Temple. With eight nights to celebrate, it's common for people to pick at least one evening to invite friends and family for a Hanukkah dinner.

The main course can be anything, but beef brisket is popular with Jewish people whose ancestors came from Eastern Europe. It's what goes with that main course that is most important to the holiday tradition. This is where things get fried!

Latkes (page 33) are fried potato pancakes that can be served with applesauce or sour cream.

Don't forget the sweet treats! **Sufganiyot** (soof-gahn-eeyot) are jelly-filled donuts. They are a sweet, deep-fried Hanukkah tradition. They are very popular in Israel.

Sephardic Jews, who are from Spain and Portugal, make buñuelos, unfilled donuts with a sweet topping. They also make cheese pancakes called cassola and spinach or leek fritters called keftes. In Iraq, Mizrachi Jews make zengoula, funnel cakes soaked in syrup. And in India, Jewish people make pakoras and gulab jamun, balls of dough fried and dipped in syrup.

And if you're not full yet and want a Hanukkah treat that is not cooked in oil, there are always chocolate coins called **gelt** (page 29).

DECORATING FOR HANUKKAH

Blue and white are the colors of Hanukkah. When welcoming guests to dinner, it's common to use blue-and-white plates, napkins, and tablecloths. Even the candles and the menorah might be blue and white. These are the colors of the traditional prayer shawl that Jews wear during worship services. In 1948, blue and white also became the colors of the flag for the State of Israel.

As Hanukkah grew in popularity, designers looked to see what colors were used by the Jewish people. Blue and white became the colors of Hanukkah and the perfect colors to use for decorations at the festive meal.

ACTS OF TZEDAKAH

Hanukkah is a time for helping others. In Judaism, tzedakah is about doing the right thing by helping people. The word *tzedakah* (tzeh-DAH-kuh) comes from the Hebrew word for **justice**. In the Bible, tzedakah requires people to take care of the poor. Today, it's not just about giving money to those in need. Tzedakah also involves doing kind things for others.

Some families try to pair an act of kindness with each candle. One night might be a gift of money to a charity. Another night might be taking old toys and clothes to a donation center. In some places, it's a tradition to plan something big and special on the fifth night. This could be something like signing up for a whole day of volunteering. Families preparing for Hanukkah can think about acts of tzedakah that would make the holiday even more meaningful.

WHEN IS HANUKKAH THIS YEAR?

The exact dates of Hanukkah change every year. This is because Hanukkah always starts on the twenty-fifth day of Kislev (kiss-lev), the ninth month in the Hebrew calendar. This is a **lunisolar calendar**, which is based on the movements of the moon and the sun. The modern calendar used by most people around the world is based only on the sun. In the Hebrew calendar, Hanukkah might be near Thanksgiving one year and at the end of December another time.

HOW TO CELEBRATE HANUKKAH

Jewish holidays start at sundown, so the candles mark the beginning of the celebration. All around the world, for eight nights in a row, Jewish people gather around their menorahs to celebrate.

LIGHT THE MENORAH

Did you figure out how many candles are needed for eight nights of Hanukkah? The answer is forty-four!

On the first night of Hanukkah, one candle is placed on the right side of the menorah and the shamash sits in its special holder. When the sun goes down,

someone lights the shamash with a match. Then the shamash is used to light the candles for that night. After placing the shamash back in its special place, don't blow out the candles. Hanukkah candles are supposed to burn all the way down or for at least thirty minutes. They are all replaced the next day.

Sephardic Jewish families whose ancestors settled in Spain and Portugal traditionally use a match to light their oil lamps instead of candles. They then light the shamash last. In this custom, none of the Hanukkah candles are used to light any others. They all get to celebrate the holiday equally.

HANUKKAH BLESSINGS AND SONGS

Blessings are things that people say to make something holy. There are many different blessings in Jewish tradition. On Hanukkah, people say blessings before lighting the menorah. There are two blessings each night, plus an extra blessing for the first night. The blessings all start with the Hebrew word *Baruch* (ברוך), which means "blessed."

The first blessing is a prayer for lighting the Hanukkah candles. The second blessing says thanks for all the amazing things that make the celebration possible. The extra blessing on the first night is called the shehecheyanu (she-hekh-ee-ya-nu). This short prayer is not only for Hanukkah. It expresses gratitude for something special, like seeing an old friend, tasting a new food, or visiting somewhere for the first time.

Once the nightly candles are lit, there is another prayer that some people chant. It's called "Hanerot Halalu" (Ha-ner-oat Ha-la-lu). This prayer declares that the holiday lights are special and sacred.

Once the blessings are done, it's time for music! There are a lot of Hanukkah songs to pick from. Some are historic, some are modern, and some are even silly!

PLAYING DREIDEL

A dreidel is a spinning top with four sides. It is used in a Hanukkah game, which is also called dreidel. It's said that children played the game when King Antiochus made Judaism illegal. Dreidel was a way for kids to have religious lessons together. If the soldiers came by, they could say they were just playing games.

Another story is that the game was brought to Jerusalem by ancient Roman soldiers. A similar game was played in England in the 1500s.

Today, the dreidel has a Hebrew letter on each of its four sides: nun (נ), gimel (ג), hay (ה), and shin (ש). Together, these letters stand for *Nes Gadol Haya Sham*, meaning "A great miracle happened there." This refers to the Hanukkah oil story. In Israel, the last letter is swapped to a pey (פ), which stands for the word *po*. It changes the phrase to "A great miracle happened *here*."

GAME TIME!

Let's play dreidel! Here are the rules.

1. Each player starts with the same number of tokens. The tokens can be beans, pennies, or gelt.

2. To start a round, everyone puts one token in the middle. This is called the pot.

3. To choose who goes first, everyone spins the dreidel. The first one to get nun gets to start the game.

4. When the spinner's dreidel falls, the Hebrew letter facing up tells the player what to do. If you get the nun, the turn immediately goes to the next person. If you get the gimel, you get everything in the pot. If you get the hay, you take half of the tokens plus one. If you get the shin, you add a new token to the pot.

5. No matter what happens with the previous turn, everyone puts another token in the pot and the next player spins the dreidel.

6. The player with the most tokens at the end of the game wins.

Play again for as many rounds as you'd like!

EXCHANGE PRESENTS

Originally, Hanukkah celebrations didn't include gifts. There's no mention of presents in any story about the Maccabees. But over thousands of years, Jewish families decided to join what their neighbors were doing during their winter celebrations, but with a Hanukkah twist. A gift is exchanged each night at home, plus gifts are given in the community. Hanukkah wrapping paper and Hanukkah cards are for sale in most stores. Saying "Happy Hanukkah" is now part of the season's greetings.

Thousands of years ago, two wise Jewish men named Hillel and Shammai had an argument. Hillel said they should light just one Hanukkah candle on the first night, two on the second, and so on. Shammai wanted to light all eight candles on the first night, and take one away each night. Today, tradition follows Hillel's idea.

AROUND THE WORLD

 anukkah started as a small Jewish holiday. It was not nearly as important as many other holidays in the Jewish religion. Over many centuries, its popularity has grown and Hanukkah is now celebrated all around the world.

The main traditions of lighting the menorah, reciting blessings, and preparing a meal are very similar from place to place. But there are also unique traditions in the different places that Jewish people live.

CELEBRATING IN ISRAEL

Israel is a country where most of the people are Jewish. On every night of Hanukkah, candles glow brightly in windows. Some houses have a special spot near the front door for the Hanukkah menorah. The Hanukkah holiday spirit is everywhere. Even in cafés, people will stop eating to light the candles together. The most popular Hanukkah food is the jelly donut, sufganiyah. Starting in November, donuts are sold everywhere. Some bakers create special flavors and decorations for the holiday.

CELEBRATING IN THE UNITED STATES

For early Jewish communities in the United States, Hanukkah wasn't a very big deal. But as Christmas celebrations became more common, Jewish people began to think about their own holiday in a different way. In the late 19th century, Hanukkah celebrations grew wildly popular in America. Musicians performed public concerts of Hanukkah music. Communities lit large menorahs outside where everyone could see them. Some families decided to decorate inside their homes or hang blue-and-white lights outside. Even now, Hanukkah in America is bigger and brighter than in other countries.

CELEBRATING IN MOROCCO

Morocco is a country in North Africa, near Spain. Jewish people have lived there for thousands of years. Some Moroccan Jewish families celebrate an extra night of Hanukkah called the day of the shamash. On the ninth night of the holiday, children go around their neighborhood and collect any leftover candles or cloth wicks. There aren't many Jewish families in Morocco today, but the kids collect enough to have a small bonfire. It's said that anyone who jumps over the bonfire will have a year of good luck.

CELEBRATING CHAG HABANOT

In some parts of North Africa, the Middle East, and Europe, Mizrahi Jews have added an extra celebration. They observe **Chag HaBanot** (kha-g ha-bah-note), also called "Eid Al Banat" or the Festival of the Daughters. This happens when the moon begins a new phase, which it always does during Hanukkah. On Chag HaBanot, women commemorate the Jewish heroine Judith. Like the Maccabees, Judith fought against a king who wanted to destroy her city and **convert** the Jewish people. Though the celebrations are different place to place, this holiday is a woman-centered celebration that mostly involves eating foods made of cheese, visiting the **synagogue**, exchanging gifts, and singing songs of victory.

THAT'S DELICIOUS!

The word *gelt* means "money" in **Yiddish**. Hanukkah gelt comes as chocolate coins wrapped in gold or silver foil. Gelt comes from an ancient tradition of giving real coins to teachers and anyone who was helpful during the year. But in the 19th century, as Jewish people moved around the world, the tradition changed. Chocolate coins were given to kids to remind them that charity is important. Sometimes gelt is used to play dreidel. Other times, they are eaten by the handful as quickly as they can be unwrapped! To get to the yummy treat, you can snap the chocolate coin in half, then peel the foil back.

CELEBRATING IN CHINA

The Kaifeng Jewish community in north-central China is one of the oldest in the world. It was founded in the 8th or 9th century by traders traveling through the area. Today, Chinese Jews celebrate like their ancestors, but they must keep their religion a secret because Judaism is not an approved religion in China. For Chinese Jews, the story of Hanukkah and the fight for religious freedom continues in a place where they cannot be free.

CELEBRATING IN FRANCE

In Southern France, there is a community that celebrates Hanukkah in a very special way. Around the wineries of Avignon, Jewish people gather on the Saturday night of the holiday. They travel house to house, enjoying wine and desserts. New **casks** of wine are opened and shared. Here, Hanukkah becomes an evening where people rejoice in the past with new traditions.

CELEBRATING DIFFERENCES

There are different kinds of Jewish people around the world. And there are different ways to practice Judaism. Some people have a very strict system of rules and laws. Other people follow the traditions in their own way. Over centuries, Jewish leaders wrote down detailed rules for Hanukkah, like making sure the candles burn for at least thirty minutes. But some families don't celebrate that way. A family might not light candles on all eight nights. Someone might not want to sing. Maybe they don't like donuts! No matter how Jewish people choose to celebrate, it's all fun because it's Hanukkah!

Who holds the world record for the most spinning dreidels? In 2018, a school in New Jersey got 1,369 tops spinning, but the result was unofficial. The official record of 734 dreidels was set by United Synagogue Youth in Pennsylvania in 2011.

CULTURE CORNER

There are many things you can do to make Hanukkah special. Decorating the house and cooking with oil are fun ways to celebrate the themes of the season. Be sure to get help from an adult when you do these activities.

POTATO LATKES

Everyone loves latkes on Hanukkah. For centuries, they weren't made from potato but rather fried cheese. In the mid-1800s, European Jews decided to cook latkes with potatoes instead. Potatoes were cheaper and there were a lot of them!

Yield: 20 latkes

Prep time: 20 minutes

Cook time: 1 hour

---

1 pound Yukon Gold potatoes

1 small yellow onion

1 large egg

2 tablespoons flour

½ cup canola oil

Applesauce, for serving

Sour cream, for serving

1. Peel the potatoes and the onion. Shred them using a food processor or a hand grater. Make sure an adult helps you with the peeling and shredding.

2. Using a cheesecloth or paper towel, squeeze out and remove as much liquid as possible from the potatoes and onion.

3. Put the potatoes and onion in a large mixing bowl. Add the egg and flour. Mix well until it thickens.

4. Ask an adult to help you heat the oil in a large pan over medium-high heat. When the oil is hot, place a quarter cup of the potato mixture in the pan. Press the mixture with the back of a spatula to gently flatten it.

continued ➤

5. Cook the latke in oil for 3½ minutes per side, until crispy and brown.

6. Place the cooked latke on a plate and cover it with a paper towel. You can also keep latkes warm by placing them on a baking sheet and transferring them to an oven set at 250°F.

7. Repeat steps 4 to 6 until you have used all the mixture.

8. Serve the latkes warm with applesauce and sour cream.

STAINED GLASS MENORAH

Part of the Hanukkah tradition is placing the menorah in the window after dark. This shares light and holiday joy with anyone passing by. You can make this colorful decoration to go in the window at any time, day or night.

Black construction paper

White pencil or chalk

Scissors

Silver tissue paper or aluminum foil

Glue stick

Colored tissue paper

1. Draw a menorah on the black paper with the white pencil or chalk. A classic Hanukkah menorah has eight candles and one raised spot in the center for the shamash.
2. Cut out the picture so it leaves a cutout shape in the black paper.
3. Glue the silver tissue paper or foil behind the cutout of the menorah.
4. Glue different-colored rectangles of tissue paper in the spaces for the candles.
5. Hang your art in the window to share the spirit of Hanukkah!

FAST AND EASY DREIDEL

You can buy a dreidel for the holiday, but making one is fast and easy. With a few supplies, you'll be playing in minutes. Try this at home, at school, or any time you want to spin!

3-inch square of cardboard

Pens

Pencil, sharpened

1. Draw a line from one corner of the cardboard to the opposite corner. Then draw a line between the two remaining corners to form an X. This will divide the space into four small triangles.

2. In each triangle, write one of the letters from the dreidel game: nun (נ), gimel (ג), hay (ה), and shin (ש).

3. Pop a pencil through the center, where the lines cross. The dreidel will spin on the pencil tip.

4. It's time to play! Turn back to page 23 for the rules of the game.

HANUKKAH GIFT WRAP

Hanukkah gifts are even more fun when they are wrapped in handmade paper. Making wrapping paper patterns with cut potatoes combines the gift-giving part of the holiday with the main ingredient of latkes! The best part of this craft is that the wrapping paper is part of the present.

Potatoes

Knife

Butcher paper or roll of white craft paper

Blue paint

Paintbrushes

1. With an adult's help, cut the potatoes in half and carve out shapes with a knife. Try making a candle, a dreidel, or a star.

2. Lay out the butcher paper or craft paper on a sturdy, flat surface.

3. Paint the raised part of the shape on the potato.

4. Use the potato as a stamp to decorate the paper.

5. When the paint is dry, use the paper to wrap gifts for friends and family.

MACCABEE GAME

What did the Maccabees wear in battle? At the time, people generally wore cloaks and sandals. They didn't have extra money for protective gear, so they had to use whatever they had at home. In this game, you can use the things you have at home to dress like a Maccabee and race against your friends.

1. Find "soldier clothes" like big T-shirts and pants that you can wear over your own clothes. Then find something that can be a shield and maybe a pool noodle for a sword. Make sure your shield and sword don't have any sharp edges!

2. Put everything you gathered into two piles. Each pile should have an even number of items.

3. Teams, or runners, start on a marker about six feet away from the piles.

4. One runner from each team has to race to the piles and get dressed as a Maccabee.

5. The player must raise the sword and make up a Maccabee battle cry of at least five words before taking off the costume and putting it back in the pile.

6. The runner races back and tags the next runner if there are more players. Whichever team or person returns to the starting mark first wins! You can use chocolate gelt for the prizes.

MAKE A MACCABEE SHIELD

The Maccabees needed shields to protect themselves. Shields also have symbols and words on them. This can tell you a lot about the soldiers. Imagine you're a Maccabee. What's on your shield?

Pen or marker

Cardboard box

Scissors

Acrylic paint

Paintbrushes

Glue or sticky tape

1. Use a pen or marker to draw a shield shape on a side of the cardboard box. It can be any shape: round, square, rectangular, or even like a dreidel.

2. Cut out the shield.

3. Paint your shield with fun Hanukkah designs or slogans that are meant to scare your enemies away from the ancient Temple.

4. Out of the scraps of cardboard, cut two long rectangles that you can use as handles.

5. Let the paint dry, then use glue or tape to attach the handles. If you're using glue, let it dry.

You are ready to join the Maccabees and defend the Jewish people. Good luck!

LEARN TO SAY IT!

Here's how to wish someone a happy Hanukkah in other countries. Hebrew is the most common language to wish each other holiday greetings, no matter where someone is in the world.

HAPPY HANUKKAH - IN HEBREW

חנוכה שמח **Hanukkah sameach**

HAPPY FESTIVAL OF LIGHTS - IN HEBREW

חג אורים שמח **Chag urim sameach**

HAPPY HOLIDAY - IN HEBREW

חג שמח **Chag sameach**

IN YIDDISH	**A Lichtiger Hanukkah**
IN SPANISH	**¡Feliz janucá!**
IN POLISH	**Wesołej Chanuki!**
IN KOREAN	즐거운 하누카 되세요! **JeulGeoUn HaNuKa DoaeSeYo**
IN RUSSIAN	С ханукой! **S HA-noo-kai**

GLOSSARY

Bible: "Tanakh" in Hebrew, a collection of sacred texts comprising three main parts: Torah, Nevi'im (Prophets), and Ketuvim (Writings)

candelabra: A multi-branched candlestick or candleholder

cask: A barrel

Chag HaBanot: A Hanukkah celebration for women known as the Festival of the Daughters

convert: To change religion or other beliefs

gelt: Chocolate coins wrapped in foil

hanukkiah: A nine-branched candlestick used specifically for the holiday of Hanukkah

Hebrew: A language that is both ancient and modern

high priest: The chief religious leader in historic Judaism

illegal: Forbidden by law

Jewish: With a historic, cultural, spiritual, or religious connection to Judaism

Judaism: The culture and religion of the Jewish people

justice: Fair treatment

latkes: Small fried pancakes, typically made from grated potato and onion

lunisolar calendar: A calendar based on the phases of the moon and the movement of the sun

menorah: A seven- or nine-branched oil lamp or candleholder used in Jewish practice. The seven-branched menorah was used in the Temple. The nine-branched Hanukkah menorah, also called a hanukkiah, is used to celebrate Hanukkah.

rebels: People who resist authority

sects: Groups within an organized religion who recognize different teachings or practices

Seleucid: The family that ruled over Syria and a great part of western Asia from 312 to 64 BCE

shamash: The helper candle that is used to light the other flames in a hanukkiah

sufganiyot: Jelly-filled donuts eaten during Hanukkah

Sukkot: A harvest festival celebrated in autumn

synagogue: A Jewish house of worship

Talmud: A written compilation of ancient Jewish law, as well as the teachings, analysis, and commentary of thousands of rabbis over hundreds of years, up to 500 CE

wick: A strip of material that soaks up fuel to light a candle or lamp

Yiddish: A Jewish language that originated in Europe

RESOURCES

BOOKS

Chanukah Lights by Michael J. Rosen

Hanukkah Around the World by Tami Lehman-Wilzig

Hanukkah Moon by Deborah da Costa

The Ninth Night of Hanukkah by Erica S. Perl

WEBSITES

Hanukkah blessings (page 20) can be heard here:

kveller.com/article/the-hanukkah-blessings

Hanukkah songs can be found here:

youtube.com/watch?v=b-_N1qXozkQ

parents.com/holiday/hanukkah/hanukkah-songs
-for-kids

**BimBam has a good selection of Jewish history
and holiday videos:**

youtube.com/watch?v=VvFqBimGuIQ

PJ Library Hanukkah Hub

pjlibrary.org/hanukkah

ACKNOWLEDGMENTS

To the teachers at Hebrew Union College-Jewish Institute of Religion who opened my mind and sparked my love for stories.

ABOUT THE AUTHOR

 *New York Times* best-selling author **Stacia Deutsch** has written more than 300 children's books. Stacia is also an ordained Reform rabbi who has worked in Jewish communities in California, Ohio, and Indiana. She now lives on a ranch with her husband, four horses, three dogs, and a silly cat. Find her online at StaciaDeutsch.com, on Instagram at @staciadeutsch_writes, and on Facebook at Facebook.com/staciadeutsch.

ABOUT THE ILLUSTRATOR

 **Annita Soble**'s illustrations have appeared in a wide array of media, including magazines, greeting cards, and animations. She lives with her husband and their five children in Brooklyn, New York. Find her online at AnnitaSoble.com and on Instagram @AnnitaSobleWorks.